Contents

The Horrors Handbook

Here are instructions for making a whole collection of nasty things, including staring eyes, giant teeth and hairy warts. Eric Kenneway tells you how to (apparently) slice off your thumb, tear off a fingernail and do disgusting things with your nose – all guaranteed to make parents and friends shudder with horror.

Eric Kenneway is an origami expert who has written a number of books on this and related subjects for both children and adults. His work has been translated into four languages. *Paper Shapes*, *Paper Fun*, *Magic Toys*, *Tricks and Illusions* and *Fingers, Knuckles and Thumbs* are his other Beaver titles.

THE
HORRORS
HANDBOOK

HANDS OFF!

GARFIELD. ©1978 United Feature Syndicate, Inc.

JIM DAVIS

THIS BOOK BELONGS TO

Antoinette Bromley

A Beaver Original
Published by Arrow Books Limited
17-21 Conway Street, London W1P 6JD
An imprint of the Hutchinson Publishing Group
London Melbourne Sydney Auckland Johannesburg
and agencies throughout the world

First published in 1983
© Copyright text Eric Kenneway 1983
© Copyright illustrations The Hutchinson Publishing Group 1983

Set in Times
Printed and bound in Great Britain by
Anchor Brendon Ltd, Tiptree, Essex

ISBN 0 600 20744 7

Introduction

The word 'horror' comes from the Latin word *horrere* which means to make your hair stand on end. Perhaps there are not many items in this book which will really stand your hair on end, but there are plenty which should give you a shiver – and a smile at the same time.

The items at the beginning of the book are ideas for you to try when you are by yourself. The later items are mostly tricks, jokes and entertainments which you might want to try out on some of your family and friends. In the case of practical jokes, pick your victims with care: choose people who are likely to enjoy the joke as much as yourself – and don't be surprised later on if they try to catch you out in a similar way.

Some ideas for making masks and other novelties are also included. Try to develop your own ideas when making these. Always tidy up after working on such projects and remember to keep your cutting tools in a safe place out of the reach of small brothers and sisters.

Horrify yourself

One staring eye

You will need:
an eggshell
paint or washable felt-tip pens

1 When next you have a boiled egg, don't crack it open with a spoon but slice the top off neatly and save the shell of this top part.

2 On the outside of the shell, draw and fill in a coloured circle with paint or ink marker, preferably in a colour to match your own eyes. Put a large black dot in the middle of your circle, so that your 'eye' has a pupil.

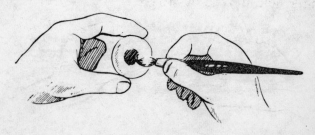

3 Hold the false eye, as it has become, between brow and cheek (in the same way as you would wear a monocle) and you appear to have one horrible staring eye.

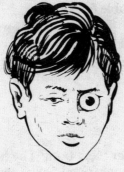

Two staring eyes

You will need:
two eggshell tops
paint or washable felt-tip pens
a pin

1 Collect two eggshell tops, in the same way that you prepared for *One staring eye* (opposite). This time place the shells on a flat surface and prick a little hole into each with a pin.

2 Now transform the shells into false eyes by drawing coloured circles . . .

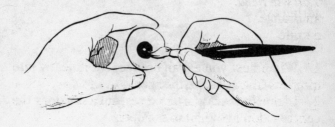

3 . . . and wear them both. The holes enable you to see. Watch your friends' expressions. Seeing you like this should make their eyes pop too!

Giant teeth

You will need:
an orange
a knife

1   When next you eat an orange, cut it neatly into quarters first and save the skin.
2   In one of your quarter pieces, cut a slit along the centre – don't go right to the ends.
3   Then cut a series of slits across the central slit.

4 Push against the outside of the skin so that the curve turns inside out. This produces a magnificent set of giant teeth . . .

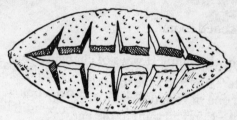

5 . . . which you can slip into your mouth like this.

Eerie light

You will need:
a torch
a darkened room

One of the simplest ways of changing your appearance, to make it look eerie, is by holding a torch to your chin so that your face is lit from below.

This is because we are much more used to seeing our faces lit from above, either by the sun or by an electric light. When our faces are lit from below, the parts which are normally light are thrown into shadow and the parts which are normally shadowed are light. The eyes look larger, and give a sickly, ghostlike appearance to the whole face.

Hairy warts

You will need:
a scrap of bread
a drop of milk
hairs

1   A scrap of dry bread can be moulded rather like clay or other modelling material. You may need to add just a drop of milk if the bread is too crumbly. Take a small piece . . .

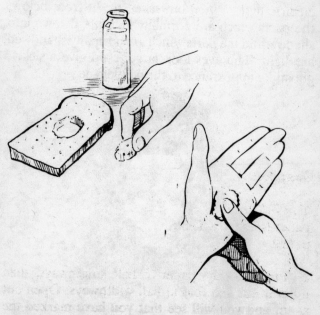

2   . . . and mould it in your hands. When the consistency seems right, break off a few pellets . . .

3 . . . and stick them to your nose and chin. These 'warts' will look more horrible if you stick one or two hairs into them. You can try taking hair from your head or, better still, use bristles from an old broom or toothbrush.

Snappers

You will need:
paper (about 6 × 12cm)
pencil

1 First fold the paper in half lengthways, then open it out and fold in half widthways. Open out again and you will see that you have marked the centre lines. With the paper opened, draw rows of teeth along the top and bottom edges. Turn the paper over.

2 Fold the top and bottom edges forward to reveal the teeth.

3 Fold creases between the centre lines to make a diamond shape as shown.

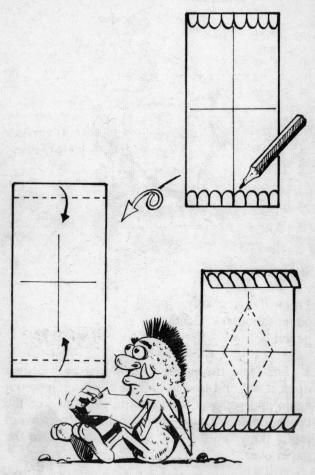

4 Now push in the centre point behind so that the creases form this shape. Squeeze gently at the sides . . .

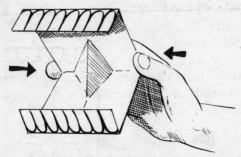

5 . . . and the teeth will come together with a snap. (For a nice 'snap' sound, use good quality, crisp paper.)

Witches' brew

You will need:
vinegar
bicarbonate of soda
a dish and spoon

1   Take a dish (a saucer will do) and pour into it a few spoonfuls of bicarbonate of soda. Then add a little vinegar.

2   The mixture will froth and bubble in a most satisfying way. (It would not be a good idea to taste it – it is revolting!)

Witch's hat

You will need:
newspaper
black paper
pencil
string or thread
sticky tape and/or glue
scissors

A single page from a large newspaper (or a double page from a small one) is about the right size for making a crown for your hat. It is better to try making one out of newspaper first before using the black paper for a final version.

1   Tie a piece of string to your pencil. Measure the string along the bottom edge of your paper and with your thumb, or a pin, holding the string in one corner, draw an arc.
2   Cut along the line you have drawn.

 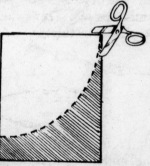

3 Bring the two straight edges together . . .
4 Overlap them slightly and fasten together.

5 To form the brim, stand the pointed crown in the middle of another sheet of paper and draw around it. Remove the crown and draw a full circle around the one you have just drawn.

6 Cut out the brim.

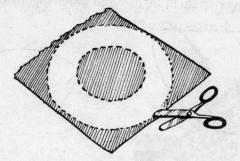

7 Cut slits into the crown, around the base, to form little flaps . . .

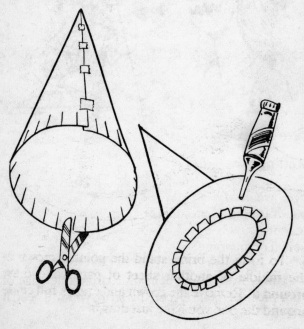

8 . . . which you stick to the underside of the brim.

9 Wear your witch's hat with a paper mask as described on pages 31–3.

Rolling eyes

You will need:
paper (about 15cm square)
scissors
pencil or crayon

1 Cut a strip, about 3cm wide, from one edge of your piece of paper. Keep this strip, you will need it later!

2 Draw a fierce face on the larger piece. Draw large circles for eyes.

3   Cut out the eyes; then cut slits, about 4cm long, on either side of the eye-holes.

4   Weave the spare strip of paper through these two slits so that it lies behind the eye-holes. Now draw eyes on the strip.

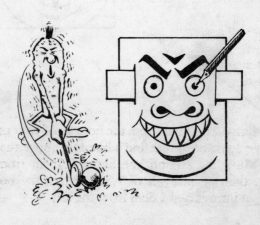

5   Move the strip about – to left and right, up and down and around, to make your face roll its eyes in apparent fury.

Werewolf: claws and fangs

You will need:
paper
pencil and ruler
scissors
glue

1   Draw a line 1cm from the bottom of your paper; a line 3cm above that and a line 1cm above that.
2   Mark the second line about 0.75cm from the left, then at intervals of 1.5cm. Mark the bottom line at intervals of 1.5cm from the left.

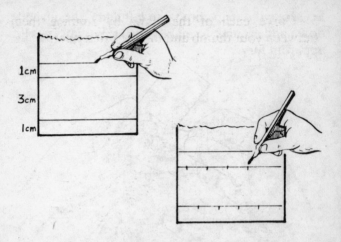

3 Join up these points to make a zig-zag line.
4 Cut into the angles of the zig-zag; then cut along the zig-zag line to make a set of twelve similar shapes which will provide you with both claws and fangs.

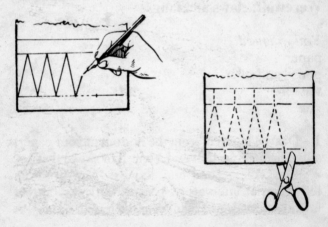

5 Curve each of the claws by running them between your thumb and the edge of a ruler.

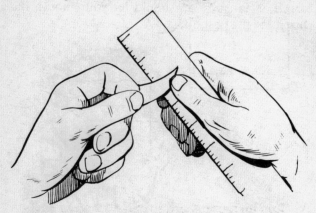

6 Then apply a spot of glue to the straight ends . . .

7 . . . and stick them to your own fingernails. Two of these shapes tucked under your upper lip will serve as fangs. You should let your mouth hang open for the best effect.

Paper masks

You will need:
paper and pencil
scissors
sticky tape and/or glue
string
paint or washable felt-tip pens

1 Fold a sheet of paper, about 20 × 25cm, in half lengthways. Cut the outer corners, to curve them, and unfold.
2 Cut a slit at the top and three at the bottom as shown in the diagram.
3 Overlap the cut edges and glue them, or fasten them with sticky tape, to raise the form of the mask.

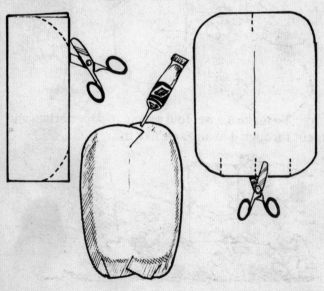

4 Test the fit of the mask by placing it over your face; trim it down if necessary. Feel through the mask for your eyes and mark their position.

5 Cut out holes for eyes. Make further holes at the sides of the mask for string. (If you fasten a bit of sticky tape to the edge of the mask here and cut the holes through both tape and paper, this will help prevent the paper around the holes tearing when it comes under strain.)

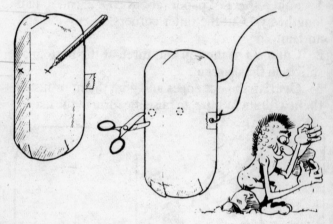

6 To make a nose, fold a scrap of paper in half and cut through it at an angle like this.

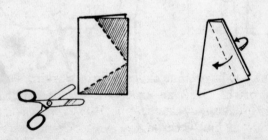

7 Fold the longest edges to front and back as shown.

8 Glue the nose to the mask and complete it to your taste by decorating with paint or felt-tip pens.

False nose

You will need:
modelling clay or similar material
board
newspaper
paste
spoon
string
paint
skewer

Perhaps you have some experience of working with papier mâché. It is an excellent way of making strong, lifelike models cheaply. However, it must be admitted that a certain amount of patience is needed. If you try to rush it the results may not be very good. A common mistake is to attempt a model which is too large and so takes a long time to complete properly and becomes boring to do.

It is better to start with something simple – and what better subject than a false nose for you to wear.

1 Start by modelling a nose in clay or some similar material on a board. Let it fill an area about 5cm square.

2 Then cover the surface with paste.

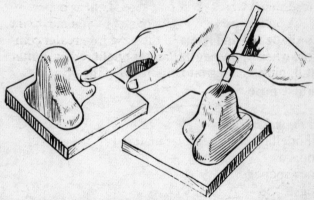

3 Tear strips from a sheet of newspaper; then tear pieces from the strips as you need them and stick them to the surface of your clay nose. Cover every part of the clay, and make sure that the pieces overlap. Having covered the surface with paper pieces once, paste it over again and repeat the process of covering the surface with overlapping pieces of paper. Repeat until the clay is covered with ten layers of paper. Let it dry.

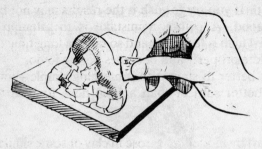

4   Remove the model, both clay and paper, from the board and scoop the clay away from the back with a spoon. You should be left with a strong, rigid nose shape which is, of course, as light as paper.

5   You can cut into it with scissors – you may want to shape the underside of the nose for greater comfort when you wear it. Paint it bright red or, better still, pink shading into bright red at the tip.

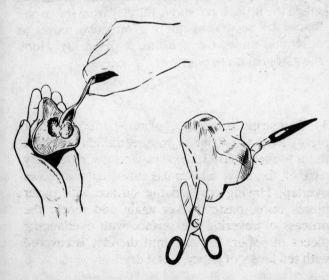

6   Make a small hole each side with a skewer, and thread string through. The strings are tied together behind your head to keep your nose in position.

7   You may like to try making some other false features in papier mâché. What about a giant ear? Make the clay model for it in the same way as you made the nose, but remove the clay from the papier mâché by separating the ear into two halves as described under *Carnival heads* (page 38). Hook the giant ear on to your own.

Papier mâché masks

You will need:
materials as for *False nose* (page 33)

Masks can be made in papier mâché in a similar way to the false nose and ear. It takes longer to make a papier mâché mask than to make a simple paper one (page 31) but it should last longer, have a better shape and be more splendid in every way.

The illustration is just a guide for getting started on your clay model base. Don't be afraid to exaggerate the size and roundness of the features.

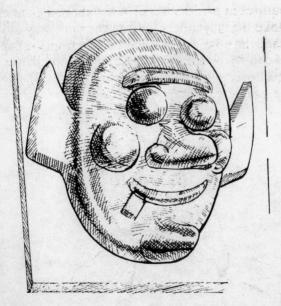

Carnival heads

You will need:
materials as for *False nose* (page 33)
but more of them

Making papier mâché carnival heads is a much
bigger task. Proceed as for the false nose and ear
but instead of modelling entirely in clay you may
prefer to find some basic shape, such as a large pot
or bowl, on which to build up your clay model.

1   Because models of this type are made in the
round, when you have finished the papier mâché
process you cannot scoop clay out in quite the same
way as with the open-backed false nose and masks.
You will have to cut through the dried papier
mâché while the clay remains inside. In this way
the papier mâché head can be separated into two
halves.

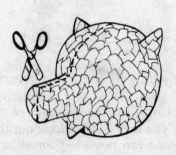

2 With the clay removed, the two halves can be rejoined with sticky tape. This will become hidden when the head is painted.

3 In some instances, where the head has a more complex shape, it may be necessary to cut it into three parts to remove all the clay inside.

4 Cut away plenty of room at the bottom to allow your head to enter; and as your eyes are unlikely to be on a level with the painted eyes of the papier mâché head, you may have to look out through its mouth – or you can provide yourself with secret eye-holes hidden among the painted surface decoration.

Horrify your family and friends

Rattlesnake

You will need:
a strip of paper (about 2 × 25cm or longer)

1   Hold the strip of paper (a piece torn from a newspaper will do) in your mouth by placing one end well down behind your lower lip. Let it hang from your mouth like a long tongue.

2   Simply blow and the 'tongue' will lift into the air and flutter rapidly. This produces a loud rattling noise. Your friends may wonder how you do it. Of course, if they try by holding a strip of paper between their two lips or teeth, it just won't work.

Leaky roof

You will need:
a scrap of paper

1 Hold a scrap of paper as shown in the diagram; rub your second finger against your forefinger and it will hit the paper with a snap.

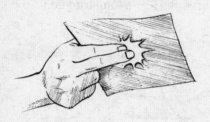

2 Try walking around the room doing this and it will sound as if drops of water are falling from the ceiling and hitting the paper. See if you can convince others that the roof must be leaking badly.

Cracked mirror

You will need:
a wall mirror
a piece of soap

1 Try drawing cracks on a wall mirror with a piece of soap . . .

2 . . . and wait to see whether you have convinced others that the mirror really is cracked.

Poltergeists

You will need:
Puffed Wheat
a plastic spoon
woollen material

This trick will not work on dull, damp days; the atmosphere needs to be quite dry.

1   Secretly rub your plastic spoon vigorously with some woollen material (which might be provided by an article of clothing you're wearing).

2   Hold the spoon above the (dry) Puffed Wheat and watch the wheat jump up to the spoon, then jump away. Electric forces are responsible, but you could claim not to understand what's going on and put the blame on poltergeists.

Poltergeists are invisible beings or ghosts which are said to be responsible for throwing things about.

Torn-off thumbnail

You will need:
a candle

1 Allow a few drops of wax to drop from a lighted candle on to your thumbnail.

2 Then press down and spread the wax so that it forms a shell over your nail when it dries – a sort of second thumbnail.

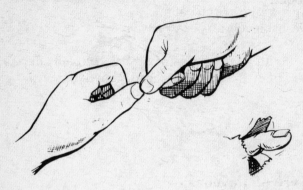

3 With many grunts and grimaces, you can now pick at your 'thumbnail' until it comes right off (actually it comes off quite easily). Offer it to your friends.

No forehead

You will need:
a grown-up's overcoat
washable felt-tip pen or lipstick

1   With a felt-tip pen or lipstick, carefully draw a pair of eyes on your forehead, above your own.

2   Now take a grown-up's overcoat and put the arms in the pockets. Wear the coat with your arms inside, holding the collar up high so that it conceals your own features. Walk into a room where there are people and they may wonder who is this strange creature with the staring eyes and no forehead.

The fortune teller

You will need:
to be outdoors (in a park or playground)
a victim

You know that some people claim to be able to see into the future by using all sorts of curious techniques – by reading the lines on the palm of the hand, by studying the bumps on the back of the head, even by looking at the patterns made by tea leaves left in a cup and so on. Here is a new technique – one which is guaranteed to produce an accurate forecast of a future event.

1   In conversation with a friend, bring up the subject of fortune telling and mention that you know of a technique for telling fortunes by reading the wrinkles inside a person's shoes. If you are persuasive enough, he may be eager to offer his shoe to you for a reading (this is more satisfactory than having to ask him outright to take off one of his shoes).

Study the shoe carefully and say, 'Hmm, I can see that you will soon be going on a long journey . . .

2   . . . then throw the shoe as far as you can.

Biting your tongue

You will need:
some tinned lambs' tongue
to be eating in company

1   If you have the chance, cut off the end of a piece of lamb's tongue and you will have something which looks very like a human tongue. Conceal it, perhaps in a paper handkerchief, and take it with you when you sit down at table for a meal.

2 During the meal, suddenly clap your hand (which secretly holds the piece of tongue) to your mouth and cry, 'Oh, I've bitten my tongue.' Produce the piece of tongue as if it were your own.

Mice

You will need:
modelling clay or similar material
a piece of string

1 Take a lump of modelling material and roll it into a short fat coil; then roll it so that it becomes narrower at one end.
2 Make two pellets and use them to form the mouse's ears.

3   Add a piece of string for the tail and you have a convincing model of a mouse.

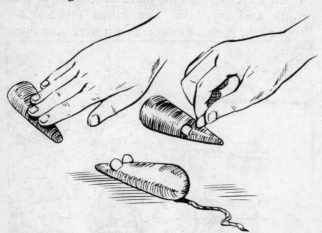

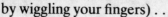

4   You can amuse your friends by letting your mouse 'run' from one hand to the other (you do this by wiggling your fingers) . . .

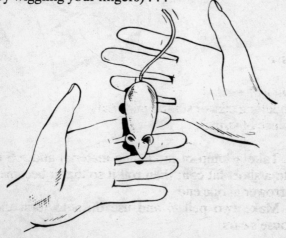

5 ... or you can leave it somewhere about your home where members of your family are likely to come across it unexpectedly. Here are a few suggestions.

Ear-wiggling mechanism

You will need:
thin string
sticky tape

There are many people who can wiggle their ears by flexing the muscles at the side of the head. If you are not one of these fortunate people but would like to be able to wiggle your ears too, here is a simple mechanism you can make which will provide you with the means of joining in.

1   Prepare two pieces of string – one about 30cm long and the other about 60cm long. Tie the longer string to the centre of the shorter one.

2   Fasten a piece of sticky tape near either end of the shorter string.

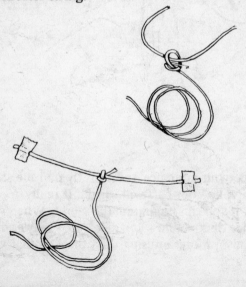

3   Now fasten the two pieces of sticky tape firmly to the backs of your ears. Allow the longer string to hang down the centre of your back. At this point you may like to put on a jacket or pullover which will help to keep the mechanism in place, and hide it from view.

4   Face your audience and secretly pull the string behind you. Your ears will wiggle. It really doesn't matter if you can't maintain the secret. When your audience discover how you did it, they may find the mechanism more amusing than the fact that your ears wiggle.

'Where's my handkerchief, Mum?'

You will need:
a piece of celery
a knife

1   Cut a small sliver from a stick of celery; shape it
and scrape the surface so that it glistens greenly.

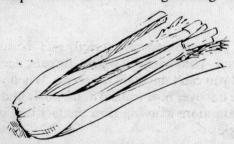

2   Let it hang from one nostril and say, 'Where's my handkerchief, Mum?'

All alive-o!

You will need:
a carrot
a knife
a goldfish bowl or tank

1   Cut a slice lengthways down the carrot, as in the picture.

2 Shape it to resemble a goldfish. A thin slice roughly shaped should be adequate, but you may like to give it a tail.

3 Conceal the carrot-fish in your hand as you dip your fingers into the goldfish bowl. With a quick movement . . .

4 . . . lift the wriggling thing, drop it into your mouth, crunch it with your teeth as though you were enjoying every bite – and swallow. It is surprising how convincing this act of eating a live fish can be. The secret is to shake the carrot-fish slightly as you lift it to your mouth; in that way it appears to be alive and trying to jump from your grasp.

Warm ice?

You will need:
a tepid drink
a piece of cellophane or acetate
a victim

1 Crumple a piece of cellophane or acetate to look like ice and drop it into a glass of tepid lemonade or similar drink.

2 Offer it to a friend as a cooling drink.

3 After a while he may wonder why the 'ice' doesn't seem to be working.

Jumping hat

You will need:
a grown-up's old hat
two rubber bands
four safety pins

1 Loop each rubber band on to a pair of safety pins, as shown in the diagram.

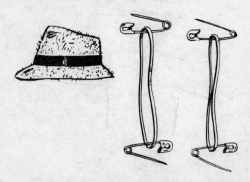

2 Fix the safety pins to the sweat band inside the hat so that the bands stretch across from side to side.

3 Now you simply put on the hat . . .

4 . . . and let go. The hat should jump right up in the air.

5 Reach up and catch the hat, if you can, so that other people will not be able to see how the trick works.

Missing finger

1 Bring a finger to your nose and, with exaggerated screwing movements, pretend to be trying to insert your finger into one nostril.

2 When your actions have caught someone else's attention, look a bit shamefaced and make as if to cover what you are doing with your other hand.

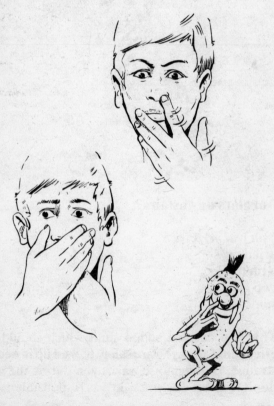

3   Remove the covering hand and show your finger apparently stuck in your nose. It seems it won't come out, no matter how hard you pull. (Of course, you simply took the opportunity to bend your finger down under cover of your other hand.)

Burglars downstairs?

You will need:
dried peas
a tin tray
two glasses
some water

This is a delayed action stunt which should take effect only after you are safely tucked up in bed. If a strange, rattling noise wakes you during the night, don't forget it was you who was responsible.

1   Before going to bed, place a tin tray upside down on top of a tumbler; then place a wine glass (or some other small container) on the tray. Fill the wine glass with dried peas and make sure you pile them high. Now fill the glass with water.

2   After some time, the peas will swell and drop, one after the other, on to the tray, making a rattling noise – or could it be a burglar trying to get in at the window?

Horned insect

You will need:
a coloured pipe cleaner
salad for dinner

1   Most pipe cleaners are made of a fluffy material and coloured white, but you can also obtain brightly coloured fluffy ones. Try to find one of these and fold it in half.

2   Twist the two ends around each other.
3   Then make a few bends along its length. You now have an insect-like object with two little horns – a caterpillar of a kind unknown to science.

4   Place your caterpillar under a lettuce leaf and wait for it to be discovered.

Some nutty ideas

You will need:
one or two walnuts
a screwdriver
paint and glue

A walnut has a scaly, wrinkled surface which suggests several ways in which it can be used for amusing effect.

1   It is a hard nut to crack but it has a seam in which there is a particularly soft place. If you can find this and push in a screwdriver there, you should be able to prise apart the two halves of the shell neatly.

2   Having eaten the kernel, save the half shells and think what you can do with them.

3   If it is the right size, a walnut shell may fit on to your nose and give it a bulbous and heavily-veined look.

4   If you paint or ink it black, the result may well look like a very large cockroach.

5   Find a thread which matches the colour of your carpet and attach it to your insect. In this way you can make it crawl across the floor while remaining at some distance from it yourself.

6   After you've eaten the kernel, you can replace it with something small and curious – a button, a bus ticket, a foreign coin, perhaps – and then stick the two halves together again to make a walnut as good as new.

7   Hide it among other nuts in a bowl and eventually someone will receive a big surprise.

Who's ruined the wallpaper?

You will need:
a scrap of white paper

1   Fold your scrap of paper in half.
2   Tear out a rough triangular shape and pleat one of the two halves.

3   Moisten the unpleated layer with your tongue and stick it to the wall of a papered room. If you place it at the right height, it will look as though someone – not you, of course – has moved a chair carelessly and ripped the wallpaper in the process.

Tummy rumbler

You will need:
two rubber bands
two paper clips
a metal washer or curtain ring
a piece of cardboard

1 Loop the rubber bands through the metal washer or ring as shown.

2 Hook each of the bands on to a paper clip. Fasten one of the clips to the top edge of a piece of cardboard towards the right; hook the other on to the bottom edge towards the left. The bands should not be taut, neither should they be very slack; trim the cardboard down to a more suitable size if necessary. Fold the cardboard in half from left to right.

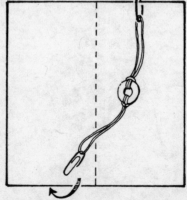

3 Now wind up the rubber bands to make them really taut; do this by twisting them between finger and thumb. When sufficiently taut, close the two layers of card and hold them together.

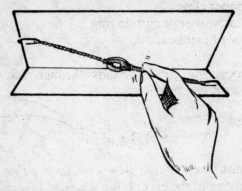

4 Hide the mechanism under your shirt or sweater. Now you are ready to say, 'I'm beginning to feel a bit hungry,' and when you secretly separate the edges of the two layers of card a loud rumbling or growling noise should be heard coming from the region of your tummy.

Self mutilation

You will need:
a small carrot
a paper napkin
scissors
a victim

Put aside your carrot for several days until it has
started to become soft and rubbery. Then it will be
ready for use in this little stunt.

1 Conceal the carrot in your fist, then show your victim the thumb of this fist.

2 Cover your fist with a paper napkin and, as you do so, push up the carrot to replace the thumb.

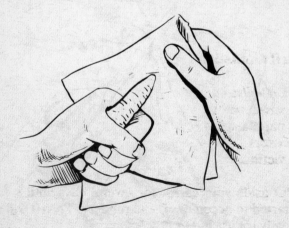

3 Offer what appears to be your thumb (it certainly feels like it) to your victim to hold.

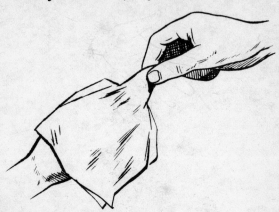

4 Then produce a pair of scissors and ask if he'll dare you to cut through your thumb. He'll probably agree.

5 So you cut the 'thumb' right off and leave your victim holding it. Ugh, what a nasty trick!

Friendly ghost

You will need:
newspaper
sticky tape
scissors
a powerful torch
wall mirror
a partner

1 Cut or tear eyes, nose and a grinning mouth in a sheet of newspaper.

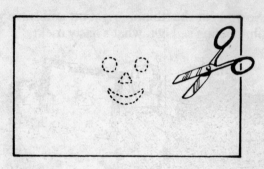

2 Fasten the newspaper to a wall mirror, covering all the glass, except for those areas seen through the cut-out features.

3 Now get your partner to stand in front of you and to one side of the mirror. Darken the room and switch on the torch to cast your partner's shadow on to the wall. Light from the torch should also reflect from the mirror on to the wall, giving the shadow eerie features. You will probably have to adjust the position of yourself, your torch, your partner or the mirror to get the features to appear just where you want them.

Once you are satisfied with the spectacle you have created, you can call in your family or friends to take a look. By moving your hand across one of the cut-out eyes on the mirror, you can make your ghost wink at them in a friendly way.

Wet sneeze

You will need:
a drink
a suitable victim

This is a stunt you can try when you are standing around with friends at a party or a popular meeting place. First make sure that you are holding a drink in your hand – a glass of water will do.

1   Pick your victim – a girl wearing a dress cut low at the back of the neck is ideal. Get behind her; dip a finger in your drink; pretend to sneeze loudly and, at the same time, flick the liquid at the target area.

2 Look innocent and someone else may be accused of having disgusting manners.

The boneless wonder

You will need:
a partner
a towel or tea cloth

1 One of you remove your shoes and roll your trousers above the knees; lie on your back with your knees raised. (You need to wear trousers for this stunt if you are a girl – you'll see why later.) The other kneel astride your partner; lean forward and rest your arms on your partner's knees.

2   From the front, the pair of you should look like one person with very short legs.

3   If you take the towel or cloth and drape it from the knees, there is a greater illusion of a single figure. It looks rather like someone wearing a skirt.

4　If you use a check patterned tea cloth, it may pass as a kilt. The two of you can then improvise a highland fling – one rapidly moving his/her feet and the other making suitable bagpipe noises.

5　The little dance is really only a preliminary act before your main performance which starts now. Lift the towel or cloth and drape it so that it conceals the 'join' at the waist of your figure; then start a series of poses. The person who forms the head and arms should take the lead in this, lifting and placing the legs where he/she wants them. (Now you see why you need trousers if you are the 'legs'!) You might start by placing one leg across the other as shown on the next page . . .

6 . . . then lift both legs high in the air . . .

7 . . . and finally tuck one, or perhaps both, of 'your' legs behind your neck. See what other striking poses you can create.

The man who survived the French Revolution

You will need:
a table with a tablecloth
washable felt-tip pens or cosmetics
a comb
a hat
a partner

This is a performance rather like *The boneless wonder* (page 83). That is to say, you need to prepare it in private, if you can, then invite your family and friends into the room to see the result.

1   Get your partner to lie flat on the floor under a table with chin up and head well back so that his/her face is nearly vertical. Drape the tablecloth from the table so that only the head, upside down, is visible. Now cover your partner's chin with a hat, draw a mouth on the forehead, comb out the hair to resemble a beard and you have the beginnings of an entirely new face – one belonging to a head which seems to have no body. With cosmetics you will also be able to draw in a new nose and rosy cheeks.

2   Invite everybody into the room to see this amazing phenomenon – a head which lives without a body. Get your partner to wink and wrinkle his/her forehead to make the 'mouth' move. If you are good at telling stories, you can describe the head as the last survivor of the French Revolution – the only person to have been guillotined and live.

Crossing the Channel

You will need:
a grapefruit or orange
a tumbler
a table napkin (or other cloth)
a knife

1 This is an entertainment which dates back to Victorian times. First assemble the few items you need.

2 Arrange the cloth neatly over the tumbler as shown at the top of the page opposite.

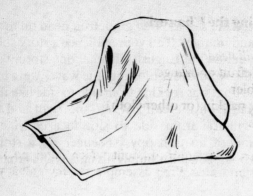

3   Cut sad-looking eyes, mouth and nose into the grapefruit; make sure that you cut right into the flesh of the fruit and remove the little pieces of skin after you have cut them away. You are now ready to start your performance.

4   Place the sad-looking grapefruit head on to the cloth and tumbler. Tell your audience a story about sailing across the English Channel one stormy day when the winds were blowing, the waves were high and the boat was rocking from side to side like this. Pull gently on the cloth at left and right and the head will roll from side to side in a convincing imitation of an unhappy passenger on a storm-tossed boat; you must supply his moans and groans.

5   Finally say, 'Oh, oh, I think he's going to be sick.' Quickly lift the grapefruit, together with the cloth, and under the guise of comforting the poor passenger with your hand on his forehead, squeezy hard. Say, 'Bring it all up, there's a good chap. You'll feel much better afterwards.'

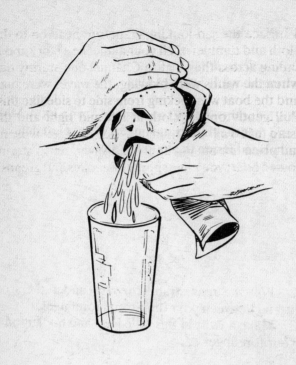

Finger slice

You will need:
string about 1.5 metres long

1   Knot the ends of the string to form a loop. Make sure that the thumb and fingers of your left hand are all placed inside the loop like this.

2   Pull the rear strand forward under the front strand between your thumb and forefinger.
3   Make a twist in this little loop and hook it on to your forefinger . . .

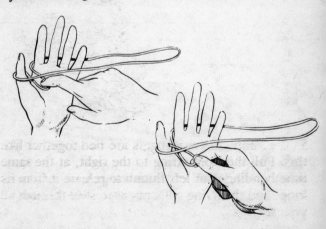

4 . . . like this. Tighten, if necessary, by pulling the back strand to the right. Now perform moves similar to steps 2 and 3 between all your other fingers, i.e. pull the back strand forward under the front strand, twist and hook on to the next finger to the right . . .

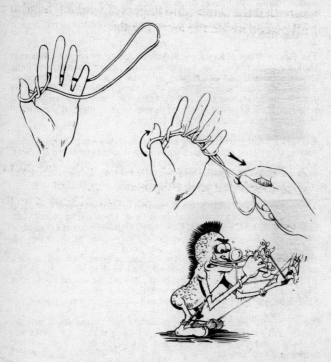

5 . . . until all your fingers are tied together like this. Pull the front string to the right, at the same time bending your left thumb to release it from its loop, and the string will appear to slice through all your fingers.

More Beaver Books

We hope you have enjoyed this Beaver Book. Here are some of the other titles:

Paper Shapes A beaver original. Eric Kenneway explains how to make basic shapes out of paper, and then how to turn them into all kinds of exciting decorations, puzzles and toys. Illustrated throughout by Alan Rogers

The Beaver Book of Revolting Rhymes A Beaver original. Whether they are about eating fleas, worms or eels, disgusting habits, gruesome details of death and destruction, or even insulting things to say to people, the poems in this book really are revolting! Collected by Jennifer and Graeme Curry, they will appeal to your worst possible sense of humour – and it is inadvisable to read them at mealtimes! Illustrated throughout by David Mostyn

Explore a Castle An exciting and original book which helps readers to work out how castles functioned and how people lived in them, including a special section on making a model castle of your own. Written by Brian Davison and illustrated throughout with black and white photographs and line drawings

These and many other Beavers are available from your local bookshop or newsagent, or can be ordered direct from: Hamlyn Paperback Cash Sales, PO Box 11, Falmouth, Cornwall TR10 9EN. Send a cheque or postal order for the price of the book plus postage at the following rates:
UK: 45p for the first book, 20p for the second book, and 14p for each additional book ordered to a maximum charge of £1.63;
BFPO and Eire: 45p for the first book, 20p for the second book, plus 14p per copy for the next 7 books and thereafter 8p per book;
OVERSEAS: 75p for the first book and 21p for each extra book.

New Beavers are published every month and if you would like the *Beaver Bulletin*, a newsletter which tells you about new books and gives a complete list of titles and prices, send a large stamped addressed envelope to:

Beaver Bulletin
Arrow Books Limited
17–21 Conway Street
London W1P 6JD

207447